The Thanksgiving Book

The Thanksgiving Book

Written and illustrated by
Frank Jupo

DODD, MEAD & COMPANY · NEW YORK

1 2 3 4 5 6 7 8 9 10

Library of Congress Cataloging in Publication Data

Jupo, Frank.
  The Thanksgiving book.

  SUMMARY: Describes Thanksgiving and harvest festival
customs around the world.
  1. Thanksgiving Day – Juvenile literature.
2. Harvest festivals – Juvenile literature. [1. Thanksgiving Day. 2. Harvest festivals] I. Title.
GT4975.J86   394.2'683   79-12201
ISBN 0-396-07703-X

"This is what I call a real Thanksgiving," said Uncle Harry as he seated himself at the head of the table. There was roast turkey with all the trimmings. There were cranberries and pumpkin pie.

And there was Grandma Jones and Aunt Millie and Cousin Paul and Cousin Pat, all gathered to celebrate the great holiday.

We spend Thanksgiving much as the Pilgrims once did a long time ago. The Pilgrims had every reason to celebrate. And they had much to be thankful for.

WHERE TO FIND GAME

Forbidden to follow their religion, the Pilgrims had left their homes in England and settled in the New World. Here they were free to worship as they pleased.

Ill-clad and ill-fed, they had braved their first winter in the new land. They were safe in their new-built homes. Moreover, some friendly Indians had offered the strangers a helping hand.

The Indians showed the Pilgrims where to fish and to hunt, and where best to plant their barley and peas. And they taught them to grow corn—a food unknown where the strangers came from.

Spring and summer had come and gone. Now it was fall and the crops were in. The rich harvest would last them for months.

HOW TO GROW CORN

The year round they had labored hard. "Now let's all thank the Lord and take a good rest," they decided.

And seated under the trees, side by side with their Indian friends, they feasted on wild turkey and venison—which is deer meat—on corn cakes and fruit.

After the meal the Pilgrims marched in parade and fired their muskets. The Indians competed in games. And they all celebrated for three days.

One of the Pilgrims wrote it all down that year of 1621. But he forgot to tell us the exact date.

THE PILGRIMS' THANKSGIVING

AN AMERICAN HOLIDAY—

CREEK

THE PEOPLE WHO SANG

CHEROKEE

THE PEOPLE WHO DANCED

NAVAJO

THE PEOPLE WHO GAVE GIFTS TO THEIR LOVED ONES

The Indian braves felt quite at home at the Pilgrims' great holiday. To celebrate the harvest was an old custom in the New World.

For ages American Indians had offered thanks to their gods—at the proper time—for providing their food.

Some honored their gods with a corn festival, some with a bean festival. Some gave thanks by singing. Others said thank you with a dance.

—LONG BEFORE THE WHITE MAN

To the Aztec Indians of ancient Mexico, the harvest festival was the event of the year. Its date was determined by their calendar.

People from afar flocked to the capital city to take part in the week-long celebration. Peasants and nobles danced in the temple square. They watched ball games or tried their skills in all kinds of sports.

Aztec celebrations were never staged without human sacrifice. So, at the height of the festival, a young girl, especially chosen, was put to death to honor the Harvest Goddess. High priests performed the sacred rite atop the temple steps with the crowds looking on.

THE PEOPLE WHO GAVE A LIVE GIFT TO THEIR GODS

THE SUN

THE RAIN

AND THE GOOD EARTH

That was many centuries ago. But harvest festivals were known even earlier. They go back to the time when Man began farming.

When people raised their first barley and their first wheat, they made a discovery: Nothing would grow without fertile soil and the sun and the rain.

In those days people believed that spirits and gods caused the sun to shine and the rain to fall.

OF SPIRITS AND GODS

BABYLON

IN CHARGE OF SUN

AFRICA

IN CHARGE OF RAIN

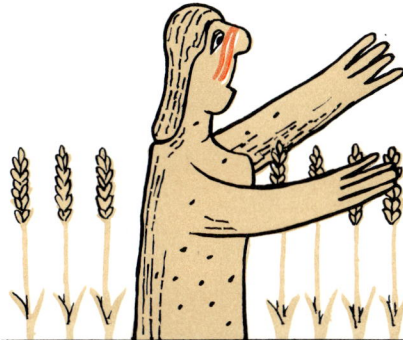

EASTERN EUROPE

IN CHARGE OF THINGS THAT GROW

So they tried to win the favor of the gods with prayers and offerings. They were grateful for the crops and gave thanks to those who—they thought—provided them.

In those long-ago days, no one knew more about farming than the people of ancient Egypt. In a country with little game to hunt, they had to depend on what their farmers could grow.

GIVING THANKS IN ANCIENT EGYPT

In spring, when the grain was ripe, the cutting done, and the granaries full, people staged a great procession to honor the God of Fertility.

At its head walked the priests, leading a sacred bull. They were followed by the royal court as the procession wound its way from the temple to a nearby field. There the last stalk was always left standing, to be cut by the King as a gift to the "Mother of the Wheat."

GIVING THANKS IN ANCIENT GREECE

OUTINGS IN THE COUNTRY

GIVING THANKS IN ANCIENT ISRAEL

The Jews of Biblical times had two harvest festivals. One in the spring—known as Shabuoth—was to give thanks for their grain. Another in the fall—called Sukkoth—was in praise of the Lord for blessing their orchards and vineyards.

In ancient Greece farmers held a great feast when the first loaf of bread was baked from the new grain.

As time passed, and farming spread, harvest festivals became common everywhere.

GIVING THANKS IN ANCIENT ROME

PROCESSIONS IN THE TOWNS

Some people thought that plants themselves were spirits. Indonesians tiptoed through their rice fields, afraid to waken the young plants.

Danish farmers often left one sheaf uncut, so that the spirits who lived in their fields would have a place to go after the harvest.

Peasants in Poland believed in a "corn spirit" in the shape of a goat. To insure good crops, they put up his likeness in their fields—all made of corn stalks to flatter him.

REGARD FOR CORN IN POLAND

THE "ERNTEKRANZ" IN AUSTRIA

The custom of making corn dolls—or corn crowns or corn wreaths—at harvest time survives to this day.

In Austria the prettiest girl is presented with an *Erntekranz*—a wreath of flowers and ears of grain. In Portugal, at a summer Thanksgiving festival, girls parade wearing harvest crowns made of loaves of bread baked from the new grain.

In Czechoslovakia some farm folk celebrate the harvest by parading through the village with the last sheaf, which they dress as an old woman—the "Corn Baba." At the end of the procession the "Baba" is drenched with water to insure a good season in the coming year.

THE "CORN BABA" IN CZECHOSLOVAKIA

A "THANK YOU"—

Though the machine has changed the farmer's life, old customs have not quite disappeared. In some parts of the world, people still celebrate harvest fairs as in days gone by.

Each autumn the townfolk of the Swiss city of Bern hold an Onion Festival. Displays of onions decorate the market square, and there is merrymaking all through the night.

Dairy farmers in the Alps have their own way of giving thanks—not for the crops from their fields but for the safe homecoming of their cattle.

—FOR ONIONS

Each spring the herds are driven up to graze in the green mountain pastures. They are driven down at summer's end.

The whole village turns out when the cattle return, flower-bedecked, dingling bells around their necks. The best milk-cow—the Queen—is in the lead.

A GREAT "THANK YOU" FOR MILK

TASTING THE NEW WINE

Then the people give thanks for the herd's safe return. Some offer a prayer in church. Some blast off a cannon kept for just such an occasion. Then there is feasting and dancing into the night, until the village band finally puts down the trumpets and the fiddles.

Where grapes are grown, people still have their Grape Harvest festivals.

For Germans, Italians, and French alike it is an occasion to sing and dance, and to sample the new wine.

WINE AND SONG IN GERMANY

—IN FRANCE

And every English child knows about the "Pearlies" who parade through London's streets on a special Sunday at harvest time. Fish and fruit vendors, the "Pearlies" are all in fanciful garb. Pearl buttons by the hundreds cover every piece of their dress. When the parade is over the couple with the most colorful costumes is crowned "Pearl King" and "Pearl Queen."

AN OLD ENGLISH CUSTOM

CELEBRATING THE RICE

Where people still grow their own food, a good crop is always worth a joyous holiday.

In India some villagers celebrate the harvest with a community meal. The favorite course is a dish known as *pengal*—little sweet dumplings made from the new rice. The sweet treat is happily shared by man and beast, and the Pengal Festival is a cherished holiday.

IN INDIA

A SWEET TREAT FOR MAN AND BEAST

Another celebration is staged on the banks of the Ganges River. Assembling at night, young girls put little lights on tiny floats and send them downstream through the dark to welcome the Harvest Goddess.

IN JAVA

In Java, when the rice has been cut, peasants hold a make-believe wedding feast with two stalks of rice as "bride" and "groom." Afterwards the "happy couple" is locked up in the village barn for an undisturbed four-week-long "honeymoon."

Japanese farmers, here and there, still pause at summer's end to pay homage to their Harvest God as their ancestors did. Some even honor their scarecrows for guarding their fields and protecting the harvest.

HONORING THE RICE GOD

IN JAPAN

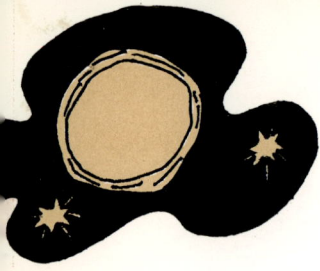

FOR SOME—MUCH PLEASURE

CHINA

Moon Cakes

TAIWAN

Everywhere old beliefs and old customs live on. People in ancient China thought that the moon caused their crops to grow. So up to this day, wherever Chinese live, come September, they observe a gay Harvest Moon Festival.

Munching moon cakes is part of the joy. Round and sweet, and decorated with a picture of the moon, the little cakes are a treat no Chinese would care to miss at this time of year.

FOR SOME—EXTRA WORK

GHANA

NIGERIA

Preparing something extra-special to eat for the harvest feast is also a custom with people all over Africa.

In Ghana, village youngsters tramp for days from house to house collecting ingredients for the harvest meal. When the great day comes, older sisters prepare the festival dinner in the public square.

Nigerians are fond of a festive dish known as *fufu*—made of yams and cassava and prepared with loving care weeks in advance.

FOR SOME IT MEANS RESTING

IVORY COAST

Many African people prepare for their festivals far ahead of the date. In some tribes men take a long rest in advance, to be at their best at the festivities. Women begin grooming themselves days before the holiday. Some adorn themselves with decorative scars. Others—for hours on end—attend to their hairdos.

Then the celebrating begins—most often with a tasty harvest feast.

YET FOR ALL—

FOR SOME IT MEANS GROOMING

UPPER VOLTA

ANGOLA

SUDAN

After the meal young and old join in a tribal dance, all the while singing and chanting or clapping their hands in time to their drums.

In between they may pause to watch wrestling matches or make-believe wild animal hunts.

Some tribes invite their ancestors' spirits to share in the fun. Others try to scare them away with blasts from their rifles.

—IT MEANS DANCING

FUN FOR THE LIVING

BARBADOS

FOOD FOR THE DEAD

HAITI

People of the islands in the Caribbean also celebrate special harvest holidays. In Barbados, the "Crop Over"—at one time a sugar harvest festival—goes on for a whole month. At the peak of the celebration cheering crowds watch the burning of a lifelike puppet that represents a much-hated plantation overseer of days long ago.

In Haiti, villagers invite all their relatives for a great harvest meal of choice yams. A portion of the dinner is put aside for their ancestors' ghosts.

Many Indians in Latin America still work their fields with digging sticks and hand plows. They toil long hours to get crops to grow.

But when the harvest is in, it is fiesta time. Then they all dress in holiday costumes and their old-time dances come alive.

Some dancers just stay in place stamping their feet. Others whirl around for days and nights.

MUSIC IN THE JUNGLE

BRAZIL

DANCING IN THE TOWNS

BOLIVIA

Some dance to tunes played on bamboo canes. Some dance to the sound of reed pipes.

Bolivian peasants perform their ancient harvest rites in front of their church. Wearing towering headdresses, they circle the village square, all the while beating their drums.

In another part of the world—in Canada—people observe Thanksgiving much as we do. But the date is different.

Canadians celebrate Thanksgiving on the second Monday in October. We have chosen the last Thursday in November for our Thanksgiving Day.

AND FOR US AT HOME—

A nationwide "Day of Thanks" was first proclaimed by George Washington in November of 1789. In 1863, Abraham Lincoln revived the custom.

But Thanksgiving days were known in America before and after the Pilgrims held their famous feast. Settlers and colonists had their own days for giving thanks whenever it suited them—for good crops, for the arrival of new immigrants, for needed supplies from overseas.

Now all America happily celebrates Thanksgiving on the same day—with prayers and turkey dinners, with family visits and grand parades.

—THE GRAND PARADE

Yet some Americans, aware of their origins, observe their own Thanksgiving besides.

Each year in late summer, the Pueblo Indians of the Southwest hold a Corn Festival. They give thanks to the Great Spirit the way their ancestors did. They hold open house and exchange gifts with friends and neighbors. In the end they perform what they call the "Green Corn Dance."

THANKS TO THE GREAT SPIRIT

Chinese-Americans celebrate their ancient Moon Harvest Festival with fierce-looking dancing dragons and fireworks and joyous crowds.

Americans of Jewish religion observe Sukkoth—their fall harvest holiday. Some build little huts from greenery wherever they can find space. Here they pray and take their meals.

The little huts are reminders of the makeshift shelters Israelites used when they wandered through the desert.

THE PUEBLO INDIANS

In Plymouth, Massachusetts, the place where the Pilgrims had their first Thanksgiving dinner, the holiday is celebrated in a fitting way.

At the stroke of five in the afternoon, townsfolk in Pilgrim dress parade through the streets to join a waiting crowd and sing Pilgrims' hymns at the site of the old Meeting House.

Though people's ways differ around the world, to pause and give thanks for their food is one custom most of them share.

THE "PILGRIMS" OF PLYMOUTH TODAY